At The End Of The Path

Theodore Edwin Hovey

Cover Photo by Theodore Edwin Hovey

ISBN: 0-9822434-4-8

Published by ReadMe Publishing
http://readme.us.com

Introduction

By Paula Berman

I know Theodore Edwin Hovey best as "Steppe", a name which perfectly fits the side of him I know, but which probably bears some explanation. In March 2008, I joined an online poetry critique forum. I spent a lot of time reading poems posted there, of widely varying quality, and I couldn't help notice one poet there, a writer whose handle was "Steppe".

Most striking were his subject matter and his style. Steppe was older (the third poem he posted is titled "I Am Old") and he was pouring out his lifetime, the things he'd seen and known both growing up and growing old, in his poems.

Over the time he's been writing, it's been a great pleasure to see the improvement in Hovey's writing; he's absorbed knowledge like a prickly pear absorbs rainwater, incorporating what he's learned into both newer work and into rewrites of his older work. When I look at them now, his oldest poems seem as polished as his newer work.

It occurs to me that the change in my
perception may be only partly due to
his own rewrites; perhaps I have also
developed "desert eyes". When you
visit a desert for the first time, it
looks unimaginably bleak; you need to
live with and in it for a time and
then suddenly it has life everywhere
and a thousand subtle shades of green.
Like the high desert, Hovey's poetry
is austere and sparse, with none of
the grandiloquent flourishes used by
poets from kinder climates. He writes
of hard times and dry land, finding
beauty in a wrinkled face with loving
eyes, a tumbledown fencepost now used
by nesting birds, or the slant of
sunlight into a deserted house. Read
this collection with "desert eyes",
looking for life in subtle and quiet
places, and you will find that Hovey's
writing is redolent of the land he's
lived in and the history he's lived
through, with the smells wind and
sage, dust and depression, defiant
life, slanting sunbeams, and hope in
each poem.

A Cross of Leaves

a cross of leaves
on the tree's steeple

greeter of wind
and friendly people

of painted birds
and purple sky

cathedral moons
floating by

Sundown

I am old
I warm myself in the weeds
my back to an ageing post
I rest-
my dreams gather

the birds
will make of my hair a nest

Over Confidence

bee glides through paws
and slanted eyes

consternation
where it flies

flits to top
of sleepy shack

smugly takes
a look at cat

feigning nap

Crickets

setting alone by the lake
among the weeds

wishing the crickets
would sing

I could live forever
in the sawed silence

of their dry chirping

A Migrant Moon

prairie dog dusk
blue wind of the plains

the desert haze
in the setting sun

a flash of hawk
a red glow from the hills

a pebbled path
a migrant moon

to guide me home

Weeds

I love the weeds
on summer days
that grows along
some country roads

where chickens peck
and children play
and lilacs bloom
among the toads

And if you follow them
they lead
to an old house
with a broken gate

where dreams and memories
wander lost
some too soon
and some to late

Juncos

heads
in their habits
like ancient monks
dark-eyed
juncos
fold their feet under
a plump
of prayers
chanting
through a long night
of winter

squatting on the cold
they fluff their feathers
spreading over
the powdery snow
like quilts

Quailness

sprints
to fields
with warm sun
and little rain

sleepy night
rising grey

topknots
heard
rejoicing

The Cradle

breeze like a child's breath
among the wheat

telephone wires that sway
only a little

and noon
napping the birds to sleep
with little peeps

A Touch of Tang

on the hill's crest
the path leads
through open portals

among huge rocks
and fragrant mists
dwell immortals

flight of birds
over the gods
and sacred breeze

I wish I too
could build a home
in a temple of trees

I Won't Complain

I will only stay here
for a little while
I seek a place perhaps
as wide as graves

It could be over there
on that little hill
where I can see the valleys
and the mountains too

I won't complain
if it is by the river
or down the meadows
by a dark or purple cloud

I will not care
if it is where the light recedes
but comes again with birds
wind waving loud

Retired

I will go
a dry thistle in my mouth
and live among the daisies
dandelions

where dreams gently glide
I could be silent there
for years

The Edge Of Night

I hear in the coolness
a flutter of wings

and feel too
those deeper stirrings

sparrows to eaves
in the flying light

with children playing
on the edge of night

Down the Road

lift blade
of grass
and see

rivers
woodlands
seas

ah
time
to travel
now

avoiding
my cluttered
cabin

In A Harsh Land

prairie lupine
arrow leaf balsamroot
buffalo plum locoweed

leopard lily
sagebrush buttercup
desert evening primrose

knowing the names
of things
makes real

their struggle
to survive

And I Miss Them

their names
in the sky
and the smoke
of the clouds
and the birds
in the wind
and the hawk
in the sun
and the geese
on their long journey home

and here
in the language of sparrows

Eastern Oregon

mountains
loom from darkness

yawn
when sleepy grey

I wake
pink clouds arrive-

dapple
the edge of day

At The End Of The Road

there at the end of the road
where the last lark sang its last song
the hawk dipped a wing
in the red glow of sunset

in the drift of ancient wood smoke
one could almost hear
a quite shifting of gears
as the prairie world turned on its
ends

suddenly an evening breeze
shuffled the edge of old memories
through the dust and pebbles of lost
dreams
and forgotten light

Second Post on the Left

past autumn sun
where shadows of night

awaken the stars
and rivers of light

larks in the meadows
owls in the trees

asleep old footprints
among scattered leaves

smoke in the valley
a house on the hill

second post on the left
is standing there still

Intangibles

the field
green

the wind
not seen

revealing
self

in waving
grass

whose lean

is proof

The Fisher

sound of reeds
on the bank

heron dips
a needle-beak

its own reflection
a prank

its lunch
bleak

Snow Bunting

in the bleak fog
a log

is rescued only
by a white of wings

and hint
of brown

snug
in a drift of snow

her grains of winter

Awakening

light
falling
through night

world
wakens
in its bird borrowed
lodgings

Keeping Busy

a barbed fence
waves its skinny fingers in the wind

and beckons birds to perch
upon a post

and as if bored with broken gates
it runs along the edges of the sky

to greet the light of early stars
and never caring never knowing why

Songs On The Meadow

in the night rises
a leafy voice

from dewy grass
new speech

If you stand listening
the starry night

will leave a song
on the meadow

Backyard Hoe-Down

swaying
shadows

beetle
stomp

round
a stump

fiddles
gather

we will all

rejoice

together

Leaving The Village

I saw the road went winding round a
long and lowering hill
attached to fences barbed with birds
and singing songs of sadness at our
passing

left alone to sulk old shoes were
shouting in the sun
while mouths of dolls went yelling in
the yards
and hatchet heads of hens and cows
were lowing in the fields

a troubled troth of tiny tears fell
terrible and long
on dandelion days we drowned
and left alone we buried them
whose bones we never found

Ebb Tide

tears
in the blink
of her dark eyes

a beak opens

sorrow laps
in the wash
of a dream

slow ebb
flowing away

with sand and seashells

    to the sea

The Blessing

mullein
lift their arms
in praise

as elevated suns
bless
the golden wheat

over the hills
the curving road
gone

No Luck

boy

fence

river:

big fish
swims

in dark
eddies-

dreams

Stillness

by the fence at dawn
a stillness
no one sees

among the grass
the windy sleep
of silent centuries

Monochrome

wheat fields
need color

they're all
gold

wind stirs
the spires-

even butterflies
need a flower

to play with

Chickadees

snow on a tree
by my window

ice whites a nest
long abandoned

on the ground
chickadees mix
in mobs of merry

their black caps warming
flanks of feathers

The Break In

house
in the frame
of the morning
a door
dark
where rising wheat
picks
the lock
enters with sheaves
of curious
yellow-

the table set for two
bids it welcome
offering a blue vase
stems and leaves
in the air

Evening Grosbeak

what
I saw
there

were yellow beak
and gold crown

evenings
wait
had whitened
a wing

Nature

beautiful passion
whistling on my shoulders

elusive are
your many dreams

siren
on the edge of green

eyes peering
from a nests of birds

The Intruder

a blue lilac
pokes
within a pane

leaves a shadow
where the sun
has stained

completing its surveillance
works with ease

and places there
a fragrance
just to please

Clothesline

what I saw
there

were thin
birds

if they were
birds

hanging by their wooden
beaks

lined across
for washday
Wednesday

For Robert Kipniss

```
leaves limn
intaglio

night falls
sfumato

tones of
the solitude

ghost like
the quietude
```

The Crystal Pool

waterwheel
paddles drop

a splash falls
on rippled top

mossy banks
align the hue

warbler dipping
crystal blue

overgrown with trees
the pool

a very very
fluffy cool

Nuthatch

bird
in the frame
of my window

nuthatch
scratches
her upside down

and tins
her drum

From My Window

tree
in the frame
of my window

a blue backdrop
hangs
in the glazed sky

where branch and leaf
stitch
the layered air-

a day long
tapestry

The Quests

evening
limns

as night
attends

who comes
then

down
the path

unlatches
the rusty gate

a door
the color of lilacs

bids them
welcome

Crepuscular

velvet tones
of soft

the half real
the half imago

as penumbra
turns inward

I see the house
the lighted window

Home

blue
the woods

steps
the moon

round which the geese
go home

then
the house

white like wings

defines
the route of birds

The Fish

a flash of wing
where fin wintered

rainbow arch
ripples splintered

eschewing hook
and slashing seam

returns to dark
and murky dream

among the stones
it reigns supreme

just an old thief
a robber of dreams

Dad's Old Cloths

his rumpled pants
lay unnoticed in a corner

incrusted with cement
as grey
as green

store bought
they sagged allot
when I tried them on

"ball room"
my father said

"room to lean"

Old man on the path

lay like
a bent
leaf

curled around
a dead
weed

knees
up
as in relief

head pillowed
on old
tweed

his last dream
a garden
green

good place
to die
it seemed

His face
grey
his smile serene

I remember
I was just
fourteen

The Hollow Hills

In the meadows
a conversation of cottonwoods
dark
with the cry of owls

mourning doves sang
in the evenings
we slept
in their sad songs

our longings for other worlds
were wings in the wind
but our childish dreams still live
in the hollow hills

House Sparrow

old world exotic
of crack
and crevice
and warm eaves

noisy
as nomads
this happy band
of hobos

Diet Time

a fat little bug clings
to the tall wheat

too plump to turn around
and journey down

he will try again
in cooler air
to reach the top

if he's not eaten
by a fat little bird

chop-chop

The Nursery

breeze
like a child's
breath
among
the wheat

telephone
wires
that sway
only
a little

and
noon
napping
the birds
to sleep
with little
peeps

I Have Been Asked

I have been asked
why I'm so quiet
in a crowd

I respond
that when mouth opens
learning stops

then there is
the gift of childhood
in the west

the prairie grass
the rolling hills
the silent rest

The Way Home

look up
from penny candles
lullabies

to neon lights
and empty streets

where all I had to eat
were stars

the weedy path
the way home

forgotten

Oneness

in our eyes-
two that make

comb of oneness
wondrous

sharing of sweet treats

slips in and out of holes

to cross-pollinate

and then renew
honey and bee

The Stuff Of Dreams

a child shivers on a stone
the broom runs to catch a fly
a barn lays a golden egg
and cattle moo the crocked sky

crows slide down slanted hook
an outhouse reads a dirty book
happy ghosts above the bed
where only dead can play with dead

poplars steal the wind's breeze
chickens peck at rusty seeds
the dog meows the cat barks
the Easter bunnies in the weeds

I know you think this makes no since
like apples growing on the fence
but when the horses drink the wine
the dream becomes both cruel and kind

Early Bird

beak
on the back
of a barked log

opens
with
vibrant need

intends
to glean
in the morning moon

assemblage
of feathers

I Will Go Now

I will go now where my youth
has been sleeping in the dust

and talk again with shadows
by the gate

I will ask them if they know
where all my dreams have gone

have I arrived too soon
or am I too late

Too Late

cruising down the road
but could not see
magpies picking hungry
the dead hare

I break a bit too late
then black and white
on blur of bees and butterflies
and window-glare

stopping by the side
and on the front
a poor bird raised its head
to look at me

but lowered it again
as if to say

I was last to leave the road
just let me be

Eastern Washington

sunset nests
in green and blue

over the wheat
with an ashen hue

reminding one
that dusk will waken

like an old photograph
that's just been taken

Encampment, Wyoming

evening
the mountains sigh

juniper trees
squat like monks

penumbra

far away
dogs bark

the last glow
from canyon walls

Those Few Seconds

reflection
the warp of what willow
what chirping meadow

along the bank and knelt
to capture it
the infant sun

opening the lens
focusing light
and then

click of fingers
little pushes
picture taken through the bushes

Open Window

over the reeds
white moon
cry of the loon

windy shore
heron bathes
in silver waves

delicate leaves
float the wind
and then descend

to table top
flowers of silk
pitchers of milk

Imprint

color plate
of light

dusk
a print of night

across the hills
evening's wipe

blue and orange
daguerreotype

Farm House

silent leanings
in the haze
dreams of sun
and calico days

mourning wind
through broken pane
old horse standing
in the rain

open doorway
waiting still
the children playing
on the hill

from mountain side
cold hand of death
to steal away
a candle's breath

Troubles

drip
of rain

on loop
of leaf

slips
to end

and drops
a flood

under the fast
of beetle's going

oozes
into

beetles
slowing

A Better Name

beetle
burrows
a black
behind
down
down
a shelter find

no
hurry
worry
wheat
is warm
name
is Stinkbug
odious
form

come
tomorrow
search
the plane
for a
somewhat
kinder
name

Patchwork

in the grey mist
as if cottonwoods
were making beautiful quilts

green leafy patches
of the rich loam

stitched
without
a sound

With The Wagoner

easy to drift
among the stars at night
where one can hide
in old images

    those soft winds rippling
    through a sea of grass
    cathedral mountains tolling
    in a blue dust

where I a scent of sage
I'd drift with Auriga

ride with him
to other worlds

their soft winds sailing
in a blue dust.

Inclement

loud
rolling
thunder

the birds
protest

a small
gathering
of feathers

low on their nest

A Gift For Mother

I came down the path
silver sage
and wild flower

yellow stems
in amber glass
arch of sunset
thru the bower

were her tears
of joy or sorrow

for my gift
or peace to borrow

Worship

pews
on the sacred arm
of the cross

crow
sparrow
host ghost

with nature's
congregation

air up there
lacks condemnation

Japan

girl
in the breeze
among tulips
lifts the hem
of her flowered dress
above her knees

kimono of peonies

the fall of pink petals
on silver grass

Quintessence

tranquility of
the curious eye
diverted from
its grandiosity

to
see
the
small

microscopically

Kittens in the Clouds

lying on my back
summer sunshine on my face
I spent the day in Monterey
away from time and hustling crowds
just watching kittens in the clouds

people sometimes laugh at me
because I care about a rose
reading poetry out loud
and watching kittens in the clouds

yet I have heard of brilliant men
who seldom dream but only scheme
to make a profit out of war
and if they dream they dream of more

I know my poem won't come to much
not like Keats or Poe and such
but maybe I can point the crowds
toward those kittens in the clouds

Voices

voices
I hear
are soft
like shadow

softer
I think
than
meadow

not
yours
or mine
or theirs

but fancy
perhaps
and
mellow

and as
they are
they come
and go

and
talk
about me-
tiptoe

Making A List

When I leave
what will be left of me

an old coat
a pair of well worn jeans

some family pictures
and a poem or two-

    and someone else
    will have to feed
    my birds

A Mystery Worlds Apart

misty stones
ancient bones
the resting place
of our beloved dead

yet somewhere
in the corners of a room
a picture lies
its yellow edges speckled
by the flies

In time
no one can tell
if once it held a sad and lonely smile
or if perchance for reasons of the
heart
the eyes contained a mystery
worlds apart

All That Remained

I stood by the road
watching a field
where the house had been

all that remained were a few old
boards
some torn cloth
and a rusty tin

handprints that were cookie crumbed
were waving
like a kite

while footprints and a chicken's wing
were scratching
in the light

My Daddy

your name drops slowly
the waiting heart
like stones we gathered from the river
and laid in a wall of memory
time out of mind

drops slowly on dreams of the valley
on weeds   and grass   and sage

and colors our hands
our jeans   our hair
with the blue and the brown
of the earth and the sky
and the dust of the roads
forever

Fowl Deception

boat's reflection
in the rip-tide

bobs and weaves
in the breeze

the gulls
still clinging
to the sunken mast

Where Memories Moments Meet

what shinning sun
has found my heart
and occupies my dream

what gleaming star
meanders soul
like ripples on a stream

what morning meadow
motions mind
to wander dark and deep

those dusty roads
and drowsy days
where memory's moments keep

At the end of the Path

at the end of a path
is a great place
to wave at birds

you must be quiet
like an old fence
or a sound unheard

perhaps a Pipit
will make your nose
a perch for the night

leaving you standing
in a weedy field
with defused light

Reusable Things

in the turkey wind
of the farm
chickens
scratch the light
uncovering
my big red S
and kryptonite

Girl Watching with a Crow

crow
on the hood
of my car

looking
south
where

long legs
are bare

yes crow
I know

I stare
and stare

August

midday sun
against the stone

flowers nod
now quite alone

no rain in site
the ground's not wet

they might still live
for hours yet

Secrets

I came upon it
sudden like
with rusty latch

gate that opened
down a field
to weedy patch

with carved stone
and lilac bush
no one to attend

the last remains
of a large red S
waving in the wind

Neglected VFW Graveyard

broken
bugles
call
among
the weeds

mouths
singing
once
now full
of seeds

battle
drums
rattle
against
old stones

strange
cadence
clicks
on
whitened bones

Backyard Archaeology

when I dug there
waters of youth
sprang forth

Captain Marvel
The Green Lantern
Big John And Sparkie

and "Tiny Bubbles"
on the sandy dial
of a Philco Radio

World's End

```
last
rays
of the sun
spreading
fan-like

caramel
coated
as candy
```

Still There

how shall I speak
that you might hear me
of the brown hills
and the grey sage
there is my heart

of dusty summers
old dirt roads
the wind in my hair

how shall I speak
that you might know
they are still there

Homeless

empty cans
of potted
meat

rancid bread
the crows
will eat

paper
beds
yellow and old

cardboard box
against
the cold

feces
scattered
in the weeds

a dule of doves
sunflower
seeds

a child's
doll
small red car

forgotten
beads
in a Mason jar

a wind blown
bush
a Christmas star

Old Friend

if the owl calls again
tell him I left
I'll not see him
by the cottonwoods
or the red barn
or the mantled moon

tell him
I'll return

he's to leave a brown feather
on the second post
near the old cabin

crossing the field
when the last sun sets
where the magic of his spread wings
swooped low on the moon

I'll wait for his aged sprit
where he picked the bones of mice
and we grew old and wise together

Summer Evening

summer evening
soft flutter of eaves
house sparrows
are the first to dream

leafy morning
the garden grieves
happy sparrows are
such little thieves

Cedar Waxwing

smooth
like nest silk
her tawny clothes

red
and picturesque
her tip of wings

mask
sharp as beaks
or bird black eyes

saint
or merely monk

a robber
in disguise

On the edges of my life

where the light bends
the field
distant
I stood by the road

around the poplars
a mystery
in the rustle of leaves
in the half-song of the lark
as the last voice of the sun
dips
below the hills

house
between the sage and river
nods in the early fall of
crow-light

where tired footprints sleep
with dust
the fence
hard by the way

The fall of night
beyond the dream
written on the edges
of my life
with old light

I became a searcher
a conjurer
a spiritual harvester

there on the road
time lighting its candle

The Boot

the boot decays
against the grass of years
the tongue
parched and white
against the bright sun
and lace
tugging at the beaks of crows
where eyelets blink
to see the rows
of grey old men
and dogs
on dusty roads

Chocolate Eyes

sunflowers
hiding seeds from thieves

and creepy spiders
building webs in leaves

hang their heads
in grey clouds
to muffle sighs

but always wink
when I walk by
with their chocolate eyes

Yellow-Headed Blackbird

sultan
of swamp

marsh
and meadow

the rusty
hinge

of unfenced
fields

courted
glamorously

females
flirt

with black
pants

and yellow
shirt

Only Half A Rainbow

only half a rainbow
now half full half bright
as if a half got stolen
by a blinking neon light

and what if we could borrow
as easily as this
whatever we're in need of
whatever is amiss

would it solve the problem
to get without the fight
or should we learn to build our own
those rainbows full of light

Comes With Mystery

gallops
the wind

a loping
grace

chasing rhythm
over the plains

then circles
the edge

of a rocky
rim

and comes with mystery
to ruffle my hair

About The Author

Theodore E. Hovey was born in Thermopolis, Wyoming in 1937. After serving a four year hitch in the U.S. Navy, he married and settled down in the San Francisco Bay Area in California.

Retiring from a sales position in 1994, he moved to the State of Washington, where he resides now.

He has been writing poems for several years, with special interest in landscape and nature poems, and poems about birds.

www.ingramcontent.com/pod-product-compliance
Lightning Source LLC
Chambersburg PA
CBHW031518040426
42445CB00009B/293